Minerals

Melissa Stewart

www.heinemann.co.uk/library
Visit our website to find out more information about Heinemann Library books.

To order:
☎ Phone 44 (0) 1865 888066
▤ Send a fax to 44 (0) 1865 314091
💻 Visit the Heinemann Bookshop at www.heinemann.co.uk/library to browse our catalogue and order online.

First published in Great Britain by Heinemann Library, Halley Court, Jordan Hill, Oxford OX2 8EJ
a division of Reed Educational and Professional Publishing Ltd. Heinemann is a registered trademark
of Reed Educational and Professional Publishing Ltd.

OXFORD MELBOURNE AUCKLAND JOHANNESBURG BLANTYRE
GABORONE IBADAN PORTSMOUTH (NH) USA CHICAGO

Produced for Heinemann Library by Editorial Directions
Designed by Ox and Company
Originated by Ambassador Litho Ltd
Printed in Hong Kong

ISBN 0 431 14374 9
06 05 04 03 02
10 9 8 7 6 5 4 3 2 1

British Library Cataloguing in Publication Data
Stewart, Melissa
  Minerals. – (Rocks and minerals)
  1. Minerals – Juvenile literature
  I. Title
  549

Acknowledgements
The Publishers would like to thank the following for permission to reproduce photographs:

Photographs ©: Cover, Tom O'Brien/International Stock; p. 4, Tom & Therisa Stack/Tom Stack & Associates; p. 5, Steve
Berman/Liaison International/Hulton Archive; p. 6, Mark A. Schneider/Visuals Unlimited, Inc.; p. 7, Brian Parker/Tom Stack
& Associates; p. 8, M. Bernsau/The Image Works; p. 9, Cameramann International, Ltd.; p. 10, Stuart Cohen/The Image
Works; p. 11, Grace Davies Photography; p. 13, G. Brad Lewis/Liaison International/Hulton Archive; p. 14, James L.
Amos/Corbis; p. 15, B. Daemmrich/The Image Works; p. 16, E. Sander/Gamma Liaison/Hulton Archive; p. 17, Tom &
Therisa Stack/Tom Stack & Associates; p. 18, David Johnson/Reed Consumer Books, Ltd.; p. 19, Mark A. Schneider/Visuals
Unlimited, Inc.; p. 20, Grace Davies Photography; p. 21, José Manuel Sanchis Calvete/Corbis; p. 22, Margot Granitsas/The
Image Works; p. 23, T.A. Natarajan/DPA/The Image Works; p. 24, NASA/The Image Works; p. 25, Grace Davies
Photography; p. 26, Francis G. Mayer/Corbis; p. 27, DeRichemond/The Image Works; p. 28, Arthur Gurmankin/Visuals
Unlimited, Inc.; p. 29, Grace Davies Photography.

Our thanks to Alan Timms and Martin Lawrence of the Natural History Museum, London for their assistance in the
preparation of this edition.

Disclaimer
All the Internet addresses (URLs) given in this book were valid at the time of going to press. However, due to the dynamic
nature of the Internet, some addresses may have changed, or sites may have changed or ceased to exist since publication.
While the author and Publishers regret any inconvenience this may cause readers, no responsibility for any such changes can
be accepted by either the author or the Publishers.

Contents

Any words appearing in the text in bold,
like this, are explained in the Glossary.

What is a mineral?

When you hear people use the word 'mineral', do you know exactly what they mean? You probably know that minerals are related to rocks. You might also know that they are sometimes dug out of mines. But it can be hard to explain exactly what a mineral is.

Gold is a mineral and a metal. It is usually dug out of mines, but flakes of gold can sometimes be found in rivers and streams.

A mineral is a natural solid material with a specific chemical makeup and structure. Gold, diamond, quartz, talc and calcite are all minerals.

Different structures

What does always having the same makeup and structure mean? Think about all the different kinds of chocolate biscuits you have eaten in your life. Some were probably thin and flat. Others might have been thick and puffy. Maybe a few had nuts mixed in.

DID YOU KNOW?

There are about 3000 kinds of minerals on the Earth, but many are very rare. A group of about 100 more common minerals combine in different ways to make most of the rocks we know.

When you make biscuits, you follow a recipe so that they will turn out just the way you like them. But even if you and a friend use exactly the same recipe, your biscuits may turn out differently. If you and your friend use different brands of butter or margarine, or different-sized eggs, your biscuit mixture will not be exactly the same. As a result, your biscuits may have different structures. Your friend's biscuits may be small and puffy, while yours may be large and flat.

Identical structures

Minerals are not like biscuits. Two samples of gold always have the same mix of ingredients in the same proportions, so they always look similar – both inside and outside. For example, diamond and graphite are both minerals made of carbon. Differences in their structures make diamond the hardest mineral and graphite one of the softest.

MINERAL MIXTURES

Different kinds of minerals join together to form rocks. Some rocks contain just one type of mineral, but most contain between two and ten minerals. Granite (above) is a rock that usually contains the minerals quartz, feldspar, and mica. Marble is a rock made of the mineral calcite.

Inside a mineral

Just as a rock is a mixture of minerals, a mineral is a mixture of **elements**. An element is a substance that contains only one kind of **atom**.

Scientists have identified more than 100 different elements on the Earth, but 99 per cent of all minerals are made up of just eight elements. These common elements have familiar names – oxygen, silicon, aluminium, iron, magnesium, calcium, potassium and sodium.

DID YOU KNOW?

Quartz combines with other minerals to form many different kinds of rocks. Quartz is found in such rocks as granite, sandstone and quartzite.

Quartz varieties

Quartz is one of the most common minerals on the Earth. It contains just two elements – silicon and oxygen. The atoms in quartz are always arranged in the same way. Quartz always has a ratio of two oxygen atoms to one silicon atom.

Pure quartz is colourless. But when a few iron atoms mix with silicon and oxygen atoms, a purple mineral called amethyst forms. When a

ALL ABOUT ATOMS

Every object in the universe that has mass and takes up space is known as **matter**. The book you are holding in your hand is matter. Your hand is matter, too, and so is the rest of your body. The chair you are sitting on is matter and so is the air you are breathing. The ancient Greeks were the first people to suggest that matter might be made up of many small particles they called atoms. For a long time, people believed that atoms were the smallest particles that make up matter. Today we know that atoms are actually made of even smaller particles, such as electrons, protons and neutrons.

few aluminium atoms mix with silicon and oxygen atoms, a grey mineral called smoky quartz forms.

Most of the time, minerals are made of a large number of atoms that have joined together to form a system of repeating units called a **crystal**. Most crystals have a regular shape and smooth, flat sides called **faces**.

Amethyst is one variety of quartz. Amethyst crystals form when a little bit of iron mixes with the silicon and oxygen atoms that make up pure quartz. The colour of a crystal can help to identify its mineral. Amethyst is also known as purple quartz.

The most common minerals

Quartz is not the only mineral that contains silicon and oxygen. In fact, 30 per cent of all known minerals contain silicon and oxygen. These minerals, called **silicates**, range in hardness from talc (the softest mineral) to topaz, which is almost as hard as diamond. Feldspar, mica, hornblende, pyroxene and olivine are all common rock-forming silicates.

Not all silicates are common, however. Topaz, garnet and tourmaline contain silicon and oxygen, but they are fairly rare. Garnet is usually a deep red stone, while topaz is usually yellow. One kind of tourmaline is called watermelon tourmaline because it is pink on the inside and green on the outside! All three minerals are often used in jewellery.

Like quartz, garnet crystals contain silicon and oxygen. Garnet comes in many colours, including red, brown, black, green and yellow.

NAME THAT MINERAL

Serpentine is a soft, greasy green or grey silicate mineral that forms the rock serpentinite. Both the mineral and the rock look scaly – like the skin of a serpent or snake.

Silicates make up about 90 per cent of the Earth's surface and 100 per cent of the **mantle**. They are also the main ingredient of the rocky surfaces of the Moon, Mercury,

Venus and Mars. Even Jupiter, Saturn, Uranus, Neptune and Pluto contain some of these minerals. Why do all the planets contain silicates? Because all the objects in our solar system formed out of the same giant cloud of dust and gases about 4.6 billion years ago.

Silicon and computers

It's lucky for us that silica is so easy to find, because it is the most important material in the microchips that run our computers. To make a silicon chip, engineers first heat quartz to separate the silicon from the oxygen. Then they grow large silicon **crystals** and slice them into thin wafers. Each wafer can be divided into hundreds of rectangle-shaped chips. Technicians **etch** microscopic circuit patterns onto each chip and place them in **ceramic** mounts. Did you know that a silicon chip smaller than a penny can run a personal computer?

MICA MAGIC

Mica is an unusual mineral because it exists as black, colourless or silvery sheets that break apart easily. Ground mica is sometimes added to paint, wallpaper, decorative tiles and Christmas decorations to make them reflect light and sparkle.

9

Is that a mineral?

You shouldn't be surprised if you have trouble understanding what people mean when they use the word mineral. Different people use the word in different ways.

For example, you have probably learned that when you eat a variety of healthy foods, you get all the vitamins and minerals your body needs to grow. But the 'minerals' needed by your body are not exactly the same as the minerals found in rocks. The minerals calcium, zinc and iron that keep your blood, skin and bones healthy will dissolve in water and do not have a repeating **crystal** structure.

Beauty and value

Gemstones, like the diamonds, sapphires and emeralds used in rings, necklaces and earrings, are minerals that have been carefully cut and

polished to bring out their natural beauty. Some gemstones are fairly common and not very valuable, but rare and hard-wearing gemstones, often called 'precious stones' are sought after for use in expensive jewellery.

Not a mineral

Not everything found in rocks is a mineral. Even though oil is mined from deep underground, it exists as a liquid, so it is not a mineral. Sand isn't a mineral either, because it doesn't always have the same chemical makeup. For example, the black sand beaches of Hawaii, Scotland and Greece are made up of tiny pieces of hardened lava. The pure white sand beaches of the Philippine Islands, on the other hand, are made up of bits of broken seashells.

The diamonds and sapphire in this necklace have been carefully cut and polished. Most sapphires are blue, but they can also be pink, green, violet, grey or yellow.

IMAGINE THAT!

Have you ever noticed a hard white or light brown material slowly building up along the inside edges of a clay flowerpot? That material is made up of minerals that have dissolved out of water. People sometimes refer to drinking water that contains a lot of dissolved minerals as 'hard water'. Drinking water with just a few dissolved minerals is called 'soft water'.

Below the surface

Just like a birthday cake, the Earth is made up of layers. Our planet's top layer – the one you walk on every day – is called the **crust**. Like the icing on a cake, it is thin compared to the layers below it.

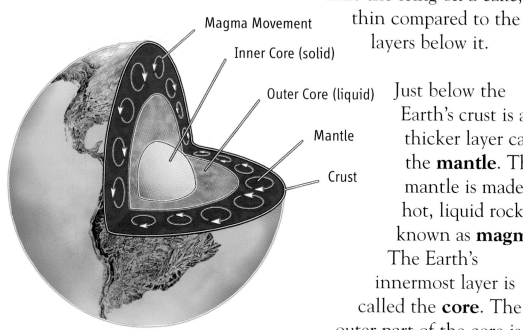

Magma Movement

Inner Core (solid)

Outer Core (liquid)

Mantle

Crust

The Earth is made up of layers. The thin outer layer of the Earth is the crust. The next layer, the mantle, is made of magma that is constantly moving. The core is made of an outer liquid layer and an inner solid core.

Just below the Earth's crust is a thicker layer called the **mantle**. The mantle is made of hot, liquid rock known as **magma**. The Earth's innermost layer is called the **core**. The outer part of the core is liquid, while the inner part is solid. Both parts of the core are made of metals – iron and nickel. All metals are **elements** that can combine to form minerals. Iron is one of the elements found in the minerals pyrite, magnetite and marcasite.

Heat and pressure

The Earth's inner core is sizzling hot – over 5000°C. Heat energy from the core moves to cooler places. As the heat moves upward, magma at the bottom of the mantle is carried toward the

Earth's surface. At the same time, cooler magma at the top of the mantle moves down to take its place. Over millions of years, magma circles slowly through the mantle.

Volcanic minerals

Sometimes magma at the top of the mantle is forced into openings in the Earth's crust and spills out onto the surface. Magma that blasts out of an erupting **volcano** is called lava. When lava cools, it forms the tiny **crystals** of feldspar, olivine, pyroxene and other minerals found in some kinds of **igneous rock**. Igneous rocks with large crystals form from magma trapped deeper underneath the crust that cools more slowly, sometimes over thousands of years.

Kilauea, the most active volcano in the world, is located on the southeastern slope of Mauna Loa in Hawaii Volcanoes National Park. Whenever it erupts, fiery hot lava flows over the land, destroying everything in its path.

What mineral is that?

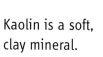

Kaolin is a soft, clay mineral.

When you walk down the street, it is easy for you to tell the difference between friends and strangers. To pick a friend out of a crowd, all you have to do is pay close attention to the way people look and how they act.

Identifying minerals

Scientists do the same thing when they try to identify minerals. Mineralogists study a mineral's **properties** – the way it looks and how it acts. For example, they look at a mineral's colour and its shininess. They also examine the mineral's form and **crystal** structure. Next, mineralogists test the mineral's hardness and observe how it breaks. They may even use their senses of smell and touch to identify minerals.

Common minerals

Kaolin is a soft, white clay that is used to make high quality china plates and cups. It is also known as china clay for this reason. Talc feels greasy and it is so soft that you can break it apart with your fingers. Halite, or table salt, is a mineral most people come across every day.

DID YOU KNOW?

A mineralogist is a scientist who studies the properties of minerals in order to identify and classify them.

Like a scientist, you can study the properties of the minerals in a rock. Look closely to examine a specimen's colour, shininess, form and hardness.

Use your senses

In many cases, you can easily observe and test a mineral the same way a scientist does. To give this a try, read the next few pages carefully. Another good way to identify a mineral sample is to get a field guide to rocks and minerals from your local library. Then you can study the photographs and read the descriptions. These books include the most common minerals and may even have maps that show you where rocks and minerals are most likely to be found.

BLAST FROM THE PAST

A German scientist named Georgius Agricola was one of the first people to study and compare the properties of different minerals. In 1546, he wrote a book describing the colour, shininess and hardness of minerals commonly found near his home.

Take a good look

When scientists find a mineral, the first thing they do is look at it very carefully. You can do the same thing with your mineral samples.

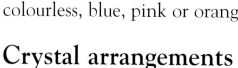

Several different minerals may be found in the same rock. In the sample above, you can easily see blue azurite crystals and green malachite crystals.

What colour is it?

Begin by looking at the colour of the **crystals**. Mineralogists know that malachite crystals are always green and azurite crystals are always blue. But the colour of a crystal isn't always enough to identify a mineral. After all, diamond crystals can be colourless, yellow, blue or even red. Topaz is usually yellow, but it can also be colourless, blue, pink or orange.

Crystal arrangements

Next, examine the arrangement of the crystals that make up the mineral. Sometimes this can provide clues to the mineral's identity. Crystals of selenite, gypsum, aragonite and staurolite sometimes form at right angles, creating a cross-shape. In fact, the name staurolite comes from the Greek word *stauros*, meaning 'cross'.

DID YOU KNOW?

Many people call the writing tip of a pencil its 'lead'. But that grey material is not really lead. It is made of the mineral graphite, which consists only of carbon atoms.

Now look at the number, shape and location of the crystal's **faces**. A quartz crystal is shaped like a hexagon. Beryl and graphite crystals are also shaped like hexagons. Crystals of halite and galena are shaped like cubes.

Is it a metal?

A mineral's shininess can also help you identify it. Metals such as gold, copper, silver and platinum reflect light well, so they always look shiny. Non-metals do not reflect light. They absorb it. That is why quartz, sulfur, talc and cinnabar look dull.

Finally, take a look at the mineral's form. Gold can come in flakes or nuggets, asbestos comes in long fibres and mica comes in thin, flat sheets.

Cube-shaped galena crystals are mixed with sphalerite in the mineral sample above. Galena is a major source of lead, while sphalerite is an important source of zinc.

IMAGINE THAT!

Beryl is a colourless mineral made of beryllium, aluminium, silicon and oxygen atoms. When just a few chromium atoms are mixed in, the mineral turns into a green emerald.

Let's get physical

Sometimes just looking at a mineral won't give you all the information you need to identify it. That's when it's time to try a few experiments.

Even though hematite varies in colour from red to brownish to black, it leaves behind a brick-red streak. It contains **atoms** of iron and oxygen.

One of the easiest experiments you can try is called a streak test. Some minerals leave behind a streak of colour when you rub them against an unglazed white porcelain tile. A mineral's streak colour is not always the same as the colour of its **crystals**. For example, a black mineral called hematite makes a brick-red streak. Chalcopyrite is a golden yellow mineral, but it leaves behind a greenish black streak.

Because a mineral always has the same crystal structure, it always breaks in the same way. For example, mica always breaks into thin sheets. Fluorite breaks in four directions and forms

DID YOU KNOW?

Sometimes scientists can identify a mineral by weighing it. Shiny metallic minerals, such as copper, usually weigh more than dull non-metals, such as talc. If you have equal-sized samples of copper and talc, the copper sample will be heavier. Gold is one of the heaviest minerals in the world.

smaller crystals shaped like pyramids. Some other minerals do not break into pieces with easily recognized shapes. Quartz is a good example of this.

Be careful!

If you decide to try tapping a mineral with a small hammer, be sure that an adult is present and that you are wearing safety glasses. You can try this test on a mineral sample from your garden or a local park, but don't try it on a piece of expensive jewellery!

Special properties

Some minerals have special properties that make them easy to identify. For example, a natural iron mineral called magnetite is magnetic – it attracts other metals. Fluorite is easy to identify because ultraviolet light makes it fluoresce, or glow in the dark. When you toss a small piece of calcite into a glass of vinegar, the mixture will start to bubble as the acid in the vinegar reacts with the calcite.

WHAT AN INVENTION!

About 2800 years ago, people living in China noticed that one end of a rock containing an iron mineral called magnetite always pointed north. Chinese sailors realized that they could use this special property to help them find their way across stormy seas. Then Chinese soldiers began using magnetite to find the best routes around tall mountains and across blazing-hot deserts. This is how the compass was invented.

When you shine ultraviolet light on fluorite, it seems to glow in the dark. In its purest form, fluorite is colourless.

How hard is that mineral?

Sometimes the easiest way to identify a mineral is by scratching it. In 1822, a German scientist named Friedrich Mohs invented a simple scale for comparing the hardness of different minerals. It was such a good system that scientists still use Mohs' scale today. You can use it, too!

Talc is so soft that it is number one on the Mohs scale. Talc is used to make crayons, paint, paper and soap.

All minerals fall somewhere along the Mohs scale. It lists the hardness of ten common minerals. Minerals with low numbers are soft and easy to scratch. Talc is so soft that it is used to make baby powder. Minerals with high numbers are very hard and difficult to scratch. The only thing hard enough to scratch a diamond is another diamond.

Mohs numbers

Gold, copper and silver are all fairly soft minerals. Each one has a Mohs number of 2 to 3. The Mohs number for magnetite is 6, while olivine is 7 and a sapphire rates 9.

An uneven scale

The Mohs scale is not an even scale. In other words, diamond is not ten times harder than talc. Actually, diamond – the hardest mineral – is 10 times harder than corundum – the second-hardest mineral on the Mohs scale.

MOHS SCALE		
MOHS NUMBER	**MINERAL**	**DESCRIPTION OF HARDNESS**
1	Talc	Can be scratched by a fingernail
2	Gypsum	Can be scratched by a fingernail
3	Calcite	Can be scratched by a copper coin
4	Fluorite	Can be scratched by glass
5	Apatite	Can be scratched by a steel knife
6	Orthoclase	Can be scratched by a steel knife
7	Quartz	Can be scratched by a steel file
8	Topaz	Can be scratched by an emery board
9	Corundum	Can be scratched by a diamond
10	Diamond	Can be scratched only by another diamond

Digging up minerals

Wherever you see rocks, there are minerals. Minerals are found in mountains, on beaches and even under your feet. Many of the minerals that people consider most valuable are mined. These include diamond, gold, topaz and copper.

Copper ores can often be found close to the Earth's surface. This copper mine in the American state of New Mexico is an open-pit mine, meaning that ore is mined on the surface, not in deep, underground shafts.

Mining metals

People also mine minerals for the metals they contain. An **ore** is any mineral that contains enough metal to be mined profitably. After ores are mined, they are usually crushed into powder, and some of the waste rock is separated out. Then the metal is removed from the remaining powder by heating and melting it, 'zapping' it with electricity or adding chemicals to the sample.

BLAST FROM THE PAST

About 7000 years ago, people living in what is now Europe began digging copper out of the ground and using it to make jewellery, tools and weapons. About 5000 years ago, they started mixing copper with tin to make bronze. Bronze is harder and stronger than copper. The period when bronze was widely used is known as the Bronze Age.

The heating process to melt down ore, known as smelting, is commonly used to separate iron from hematite or magnetite. It takes place in a blast furnace that can heat the rock to more than 1600°C. An electrical current can be used to separate aluminium from bauxite ore. When special chemicals are added to azurite or malachite, most of the ore dissolves, leaving pure copper metal behind.

Each year, millions of tonnes of ore are smelted to purify iron. Then the iron can be used to make steel, sheet metal or electromagnets.

ORES CONTAINING METALS

ORE	METAL
Azurite, bornite, chalcocite, chalcopyrite, cuprite, malachite	Copper
Bauxite	Aluminium
Cassiterite	Tin
Chromite	Chromium
Cinnabar	Mercury
Galena	Lead
Hematite, magnetite, marcasite, siderite, pyrite	Iron
Ilmenite, rutile	Titanium
Magnesite	Magnesium
Pitchblende	Uranium
Sphalerite	Zinc

How do people use minerals?

What do mirrors, radios, computers, cars, roads, jewellery, clothes and toothpaste have in common? They are all made from minerals. In fact, it is almost impossible to think of any product that doesn't contain minerals.

The SPARTAN research satellite is one of many spacecraft covered with gold foil. The gold protects the spacecraft from harmful cosmic rays.

Beautiful and useful

Gold, silver, platinum and diamonds are made into jewellery. But these minerals also have other important uses. Photographic film wouldn't work without silver. Platinum is used to make anti-pollution devices for cars. About 80 per cent of all the diamonds dug out of the ground are used to make industrial cutting equipment. Why are diamonds so good for cutting? Because nothing is harder than a diamond!

DID YOU KNOW?

When the mineral gypsum is heated, it forms a fine powder called plaster of paris. If this material is mixed with water, it can be used to make **ceramics**, models and statues. Many dentists use plaster of paris to make casts of people's teeth.

Aluminium is strong, lightweight, and does not rust. It is perfect for making bicycles, soft drink cans, cars and power cables. Stainless-steel objects are made from chromium, a metal that comes from chromite **ore**. Magnetite is a natural iron mineral that can be smelted to make magnets. They can be used in compasses, for sticking things to refrigerator doors and in industrial machinery. The uranium from pitchblende generates electricity in power stations all over the world.

These soft drink cans are made of aluminium. Aluminium does not rust because it forms a protective layer of aluminium oxide when it is exposed to the air.

Fluorite is the main source of the fluoride added to toothpaste and drinking water. It helps keep our teeth strong and healthy. Titanium is so tough and strong that it is used to build aeroplanes and spacecraft. It may also be used to colour paper, paint and plastics white. Sulphur is used to make chemicals that kill insects and to make fertilizers that help plants grow. Halite is the table salt that flavours food and borax helps to keep our clothes clean and fresh.

THAT'S INCREDIBLE!

It takes 35 different minerals just to make a television set and more than 32 to build and operate even the simplest computer.

Amazing minerals

Have you ever dreamed about finding the biggest diamond or gold nugget in the world? It would certainly be very exciting, and selling it would make you very rich!

The British Royal Sceptre contains the Star of Africa diamond. It is the largest cut diamond in the world.

Believe it or not, in 1905, a 0.6-kilogram diamond was discovered in Cullinan, South Africa. It was cut into nine large jewels and ninety-six smaller ones. The largest cut gem was named the Star of Africa. It became part of the British Royal Sceptre and is now on display at the Tower of London.

In 1869, the world's biggest gold nugget was found in Moliagul in Victoria, Australia. It weighs 71 kilograms. The largest topaz, discovered in Brazil in 1940, weighs 271 kilograms and can be seen at the American Museum of Natural History in New York City.

Stalactites

People have also found some pretty amazing mineral formations deep inside caves. When the mineral-rich waters that flow through caves **evaporate**, long, icicle-shaped stalactites sometimes grow down from the ceiling.

Stalagmites

In some caves, thick, stubby stalagmites rise up from the floor. Stalagmites often grow more than 15 metres high and 10 metres across. They usually have broad, rounded tips.

Flowers, pearls and drapes

Some caves also have beautiful 'flowers' and 'pearls' made of calcite or gypsum along the walls. Delicate mineral 'drapes' may even hang from the ceiling. Some are so thin that a person can see right through them. All these structures consist of minerals that once made up the layers of limestone that dissolved to form the cave.

Grotte du Maire is a cave in Herault, France. It features stunning stalactites and stalagmites.

WHO WERE THE FORTY-NINERS?

This story began in 1848, when a man named James Wilson Marshall found flakes of gold in a stream near what is now Sacramento, California, USA. During the next year, over 100,000 people – known as 'forty-niners' because of the year 1849 – came to California with dreams of getting rich. These prospectors came from all over the world to take part in the Californian 'gold rush'.

Mineral collecting

Now that you know a little bit about minerals
and how to identify them, you might want to try
collecting some. You can buy minerals or you
can go and look at them at a natural history
museum, but it might be more fun to hunt for
them yourself in rocks at a local park, in a field
or in the woods.

Be prepared!

Before you plan your first mineral collecting trip,
you will need to gather together a few pieces of
equipment. You will also need to learn a few
rules. When you bring the minerals or mineral-
filled rocks home, you can try some of the tests
described in this book.

You can learn a great
deal by examining
the rock and mineral
collection at a large
museum. This
collection is housed
at Harvard University
in Boston,
Massachusetts, USA.

Be systematic!

Once you have identified the minerals, you may want to create a system for labelling, organizing, and storing them. Then you will always be able to find a particular sample later. You can arrange your specimens any way you like – by colour, by **crystal** shape, by collection site or even alphabetically. As your collection grows, being organized becomes more important.

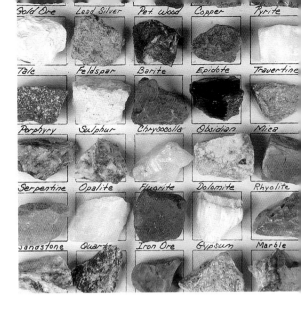

This neatly organized personal rock collection is arranged by location. You can start your own collection by sticking specimens to thick card or placing them in a box with compartments.

COLOSSAL COLLECTION

One of the largest and most interesting mineral collections in the world is on display at the National Museum of Natural History in Paris, France. The collection was started by King Louis XIII of France in the early 1600s.

WHAT YOU NEED TO KNOW

- Never go rock hunting alone. Go with a group that includes a qualified adult.
- Know how to use a map and compass.
- Always get a landowner's permission before walking on private property. If you find interesting rocks, ask the owner if you can remove them.
- Before removing samples from public land, make sure rock collecting is allowed. Many natural rock formations are protected by law.
- Respect nature. Do not hammer out samples. Do not disturb living things and do not leave litter.

WHAT YOU NEED

- Strong boots or wellies
- A map and compass
- A small paintbrush to remove dirt and extra rock chips from samples
- A camera to take photographs of rock formations
- A hand lens to get a close-up look at minerals
- A notebook for recording when and where you find each rock
- A spotter's guide to rocks and minerals.

Glossary

atom smallest unit of an element that still has all the properties of the element

ceramic made of clay

core centre of the Earth. The inner core is solid, and the outer core is liquid.

crust outer layer of the Earth

crystal repeating structure within most minerals

element substance that contains only one kind of atom

etch to engrave or draw on metal or glass

evaporate to change from a liquid to a gas

face smooth, flat side of a crystal

fossil remains or evidence of ancient life

gemstone mineral that can be cut and polished for a decorative use, such as jewellery

igneous rock kind of rock that forms when magma from the Earth's mantle cools and hardens

magma hot, liquid rock that makes up the Earth's mantle. When magma spills out onto the Earth's surface, it is called lava.

mantle layer of the Earth between the crust and outer core. It is made of rock in its liquid form, known as magma.

matter anything that takes up space as a solid, liquid or gas

ore mineral that contains enough metal to be mined profitably

property trait or characteristic that helps make identification possible

silicate mineral that contains silicon and oxygen

volcano opening in the Earth's surface that extends into the mantle

Further information

BOOKS

The Kingfisher book of planet Earth, Martin Redfern, Kingfisher, 1999

The pebble in my pocket, Meredith Hopper, Frances Lincoln, 1997

The best book of fossils, rocks and minerals, Chris Pellant, Kingfisher, 2000

Tourists rock, fossil and mineral map of Great Britain, British Geological Survey, 2000

ORGANIZATIONS

British Geological Survey
www.bgs.ac.uk
Kingsley Dunham Centre, Keyworth,
Nottingham, NG12 5GG UK

Rockwatch
www.geologist.demon.co.uk/rockwatch/
The Geologists' Association
Burlington House, Piccadilly,
London, W1V 9AG UK

The Natural History Museum
www.nhm.ac.uk
Cromwell Road,
London, SW7 5BD UK

The Geological Society of Australia
www.gsa.org.au/home
Suite 706, 301 George Street
Sydney NSW 2000
Australia

Geological Survey of Canada
www.nrcan.gc.ca/gsc/
601 Booth Street
Ottawa, Ontario
KIA 0E8
Canada

US Geological Survey (USGS)
www.usgs.gov
507 National Center
12201 Sunrise Valley Drive
Reston, Virginia 22092
USA

Index

Titles in the *Rocks and Minerals* series include:

Hardback   0 431 14370 6

Hardback   0 431 14371 4

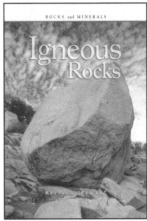

Hardback   0 431 14372 2

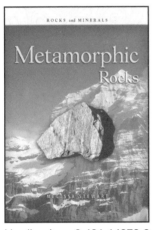

Hardback   0 431 14373 0

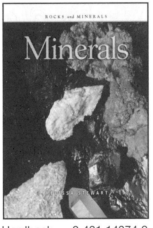

Hardback   0 431 14374 9

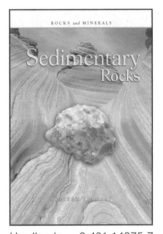

Hardback   0 431 14375 7

Hardback   0 431 14376 5

Find out about the other titles in this series on our website www.heinemann.co.uk/library